NOW

SAINT JULIAN PRESS

POETRY

PRAISE for NOW

"The abundance of Tom Simmons' imagination is matched by his tireless intellectual curiosity. A copious, ardent, richly musical book of poetry."

Robert Pinsky

"Thomas Simmons is a poet of astonishing lines that stun the page with informed candor. He has many voices and forms, all consistent with a learned poet who looks and photos world events and passion historically in ancient, modern, and experimental passages. He is the mind's astronomer. He gazes at eternal heavens fallen yet strolling on earth. I expect many new word constellations will be carrying his signature. His pen is as sharp as his eye."

Willis Barnstone, Author
Poets of the Bible: from Solomon to John of Revelation
Fred Cody Life Achievement Award

"Thomas Simmons possesses an uncanny ability to weave together in his poems elements of the past, present, and future, refracted through details that are at once quotidian and eternal. *Now* offers compelling testimony about a complicated moment in history, in the form of one man's searing indictment of the mistakes, his own and others, that have defined his singular time on earth. This book will endure."

Christopher Merrill
Self-Portrait with Dogwood

"There are two ways to transmute personal suffering: one is through spiritual practice; the other is through art. Tom Simmons wholeheartedly chooses the latter route. In this long-awaited new collection, he dives down the rabbit hole of a life suffused in deep personal disappointment to wrest from it the brilliant shards of universal longing—and ghostly light. *'With each shift,'* he writes, *'what looks like a common life, fractured and sad, becomes an altarpiece of infinite regress… fully manifest in possibility.'* To accomplish this Houdini act on an altogether ordinary life (though perhaps one 'more honored in the breach than in the observance') requires daring, objectivity, and a finely honed and totally unsentimental mastery of his poetic craft. In this brilliant debut (or better, *reboot*), Tom Simmons returns after a long absence from the writing scene to demonstrate that his early promise has indeed borne fruit. Bright, subtle, experimental, and still yearning for that unifying wholeness beneath all the random fragments, he has emerged as one of our quintessential postmodern troubadours."

Cynthia Bourgeault – *The Wisdom Way of Knowing*
The Heart of Centering Prayer – *Love Is Stronger than Death*

RISEN FROM THE SEA
Aliki Barnstone

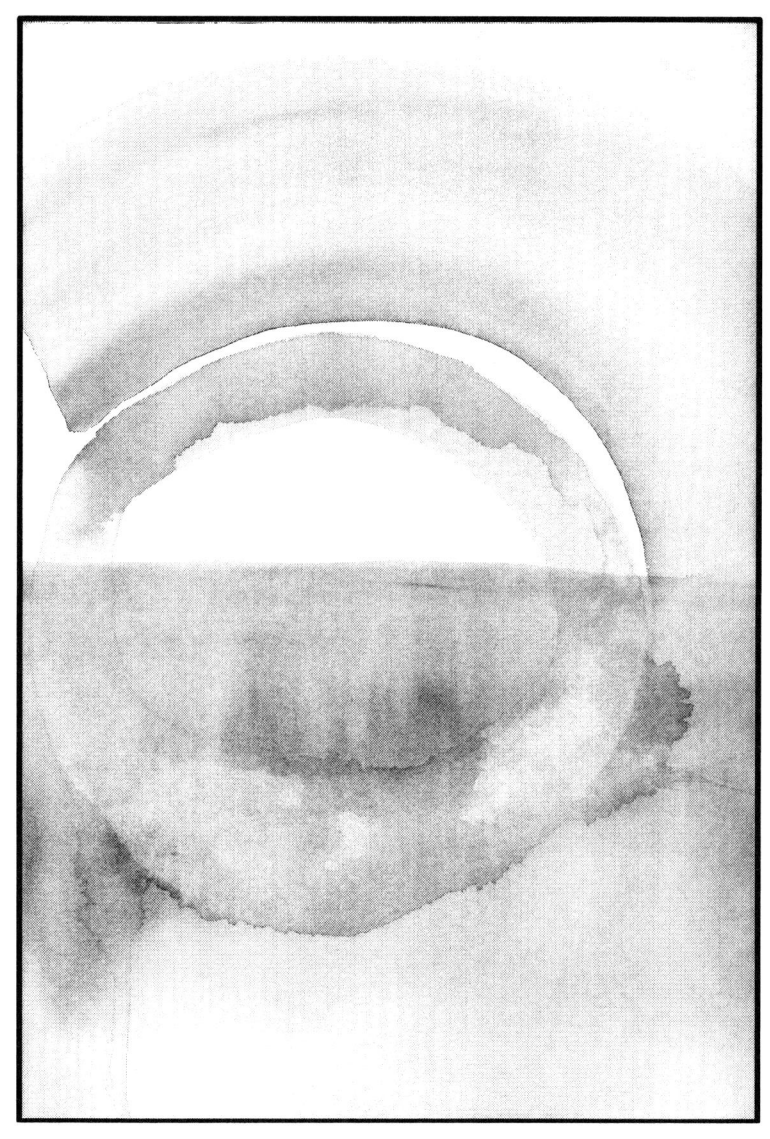

N O W

Poems

by

Thomas Simmons

SAINT JULIAN PRESS
HOUSTON

Published by

SAINT JULIAN PRESS, INC.
2053 Cortlandt, Suite 200
Houston, Texas 77008

www.saintjulianpress.com

Copyright © 2017
Two Thousand and Seventeen
© Thomas simmons

ISBN 13: 978-0-9986404-0-2
ISBN: ISBN-10: 0-9986404-0-9
Library of Congress Control Number: 2017931663

Cover & Interior Art: Aliki Barnstone

Author photograph: Self Portrait

For Aliki

CONTENTS

AN AFTERNOON AT THE BEACH

THE BODY AT REST   3

SADNESS   4

WHAT WAS THERE   5

MEND ME TO BE WELL   6

SILENT REVEL   7

FATHER   8

IF BORGES' LOVER HAD WRITTEN
"THE PLAIN SENSE OF THINGS"   9

FALLING ASLEEP OVER "ON FIRST LOOKING
INTO CHAPMAN'S HOMER"   10

AN AFTERNOON AT THE BEACH   11

THAT PHOTOGRAPH   12

NOVEMBER 29, 2016   13

THE OFFERS   14

THE STORY OF YOU   15

EVERYWHERE   16

THE RESOLUTION   17

SECLUSION   18

A LANGUAGE APPROPRIATE TO ITSELF   19

SPEECH   20

YOU   22

PRETENSE   23

FURTHER ANIMALISTIC DESERTIONS

NIENTE   27

MOVING ON   28

ARUNDEL   29

NEW YEAR'S DAY   30

CLIVEDEN 1666   31

WHAT JOHN DONNE SAID
WHAT HERBERT HEARD   32

YOU WANTED TO KNOW   33

CIRCUS ANIMALS   34

RIPRAP   35

THE BRIGHT SUN   37

TRANSLATIONS FROM THE LATIN   38

THAT OTHER STORY   39

THE VISIONARY COMPANY   40

A FABLE   41

BLESSINGS FOR A DAY   42

HOMECOMING   43

THAT ONE POINT   44

A VISION   45

WHOLLY OTHER   46

WITNESS   47

NOW

BURDENS   51

I   52

UNCONTROL   53

HIDING   54

THE BODY OF HOPE   55

SUITING UP   56

YOUR SONG   60

DARK LADY OF DNA   61

THE ARMIES ASSEMBLE   64

POEM FOR A SIXTIETH BIRTHDAY   68

NOW   69

ENCHANTED FLESH   70

A CERTAIN SLANT OF LIGHT   71

ONE SHADE OF GREY   72

SPLITTING APART   73

THE SUBTLE BODY AND THE BODY OF HOPE   74

THINGS WE TAKE FOR GRANTED   76

¿CON QUIÉN HABLO?   77

SOIL OF THE SOUL   78

CROSSING OVER   79

THE HAUNTING   80

THE LABOUR OF HANDS   81

"I spent too much time performing my violin and traveling. But the essential exercise of a composer—meditation— nothing has ever interrupted that for me. I live a permanent dream by night, by day."—Georges Enesco

NOW

AN AFTERNOON
AT THE BEACH

THE BODY AT REST

In the evening we are all of us our children,
Frightened of unconsciousness, the story's end.

This is the end of the story. Rest now.
We are inside human history, that infinitesimal

Shaft of light not yet past the Milky Way.
Forget the all in motion, forget that what we see

Shifts because we see it. Past Newton, who dreamed
Einstein but, too horrified at what he saw, dreamed

Aristotle in return, who liked things as they stayed.
The igneous rock outside his door could not be assayed

Except in its native stillness. Our stillness now.
We have fallen a long way, but see, now, how

Our mutual light recedes as our diminished sun
Appears to set. Some days it is enough to have done

Simply what we have done, and in our night
Begin to dream our journey past the speed of light.

SADNESS

It is one thing to observe the interstellar dark.
It is another thing entirely not to be observed by it,
To deduce its indifference to our being, to being—
You may say: "We make our own meaning."
I have said it. But if I answer, "Nevertheless
What I most want is someone here when I awake,"
You may well laugh at the non-sequitur,
Wondering if I am serious or, well, merely
Morose. Merely. As if sadness did not
Soar out, impervious to gravity, well
Into that most remote space, only to find
That it had outstripped itself,
That it was now merely sadness
Without a context, without a name.

WHAT WAS THERE

And when it was done,
He set it, just there, on the table,
Between the two kerosene lamps.
Invisible, indivisible, it was his heart
Returned to its primal state.

Only he could see it. People
Came and went. He lit the lamps
Each night for its sake. No matter
Whether the people knew, whether
The poem knew. Poems know nothing.

They point toward things—most of them,
Most times, within the realm of the visible,
Or something just adjacent, love or the planet
On the table. This, this was wholly other.
He had made it to defy his life's labour.

MEND ME TO BE WELL

When the earth dared finally speak to the moon,
The moon replied in kind: "We are both one another's
Shadows," it said, "and when we emerge from shade
We register the whole history of our being in light,

That first, catastrophic separation, birth and death
Of atmospheres, tectonic shifts, all our mutual scars
Now exactly the sum of what, for the time being,
Is real." The earth felt ashamed. This was wisdom

It did not want, the simple affirmation of a difference
It could not control. Who was better? Only a fool
Would claim what the earth had claimed, in its luxury,
Belligerent against the base reality of the stars.

SILENT REVEL

The deep night owl beyond your vision in sleep
Is my mastery of silent revel, my fulfilled promise
To you, no longer stranger. Hear in that soft
Voice you do not know the warranty of trust,
Your promise, though unfulfilled before, also
Made good. I do not control the image
In your head, but neither is it your image—
Only an assurance to be acted on, mine given
And yours foreseen as night shades into
Dawn, as the light rises, your eyes open to
The partial from which you turned away, and I, fully
Satisfied, fly to the high bough of my expectancy.

FATHER

To the father who played favorites, all were fodder:
Some lived; too many died, half his student pilots in the war.
He reeked vengeance: storming from attic to basement,

Smashing doors and banisters because of a minor
Soldering defect in his Heathkit, he was the end incarnate.
Also life, of course: that inescapable pivot, a hundred push-ups

Every morning, parading naked. Still I remember best a recurrent
Nightmare from childhood: one of my brother's friends,
A trumpet-player in the marching band, the boy to whom

My father applied one of his random furies, handsome,
A seducer, that boy was bricked into a basement wall
Alive and left there, the mortar slowly sealing and the air

Tinged with plaster, all human sounds receding,
The missing person, the interviews, the investigation.
It never happened. But that's where one would begin.

IF BORGES' LOVER HAD WRITTEN "THE PLAIN SENSE OF THINGS"

In love we come to one another for comfort, edification.
I heard your voice in the crowd and not another's.
Some rifts we manage—waking late, housework;
Others shatter: attorneys, courtroom, the asylum.

"The absence of the imagination had itself
To be imagined"—this does not change the spin
Of the world in space. It does not change space,
Or planetary motion, the colossal sun. And yet:

Funes ceases his memories. The Aleph goes dark.
The library of Alexandria vanishes, as it did. The man
Who dreams a man into being, who becomes aware
That he himself was dreamed—it never happened,

Or if it did, no one can recall. We come face to face
With the antithetical, the antithesis of Stevens' great
Protagonist in "The Idea of Order," the murderer
Of a certain love, the love of lovers, Stevens, Borges,

The worlds we make from this our world secure there.
Never again. How love breaks down. One person turns,
The unforeseen pendulum groans and breaks from its
Broken pivot. Forever after, the betrayed lingers there,

Caressing it with horror, uncomprehending. None of this
Should have happened. Yet it did. It did. It is what occurs
When you cannot imagine the absence of the imagination,
When you cannot remain within the plain sense of things.

FALLING ASLEEP OVER "ON FIRST LOOKING INTO CHAPMAN'S HOMER"

"Written in October 1816, on a morning after Keats had stayed up all night reading George Chapman's translation of Homer with C.C. Clarke. . ."—Jack Stillinger, *John Keats: The Complete Poems*

And age, it seemed, had brought selective narcolepsy,
Not the cheap-horror-sleep-at-the-wheel but rather
A kind of willed hypnotic state—or more, however
Indiscreet the claim—call it metempsychosis—anything
Could set it off, a view, a chill, an epic or a sonnet—
Lowell set the chariot for the flight from Carthage
To the Alps yet woke to his mother's great-aunt,
Eighty years back, and an old familial admonition
Proving as he feared that Vergil stared entirely
Beyond him, gazing at himself in the New England
Mirror—it had all be a dazzling dream. But here,
Now, Keats' thrill at the ancient text revivified,
New spirits breathed into ancient names and wine-
Dark seas, abduction, the terrible miscalculation
Of a sacrifice never finally repaid, yet nevertheless
That victory, impossible journey home, the loss of all
And then Nausicaa, presaging Ithaca. And I—
Well—here again, that young soul pouring itself
All night long across the Cyclades till dawn
Declared it mortally unwell—small price now
For "Ode on a Grecian Urn." Then, too, before;
Pious Aeneas, incredulous to find, in that painstaking
Gloom of Sibyl and of Cerberus, Dido herself,
And still herself, forever mourning. A sudden sleep,
Then, the world too much, and yet soul-shifting:
Suddenly the promise that the fate that dooms us
Also undooms us. We are summoned all at once
To start awake as those who love us all unknown.

AN AFTERNOON AT THE BEACH

"I'll go among the dead to see my friend."
—Edgar Bowers, "An Afternoon at the Beach"

Blake knew: when the living are necessarily stunned
Into silence, he dined with Isaiah and Ezekiel, who
Because they were and were not, as we are
And are not, were ever-present, happy to affirm
For Blake the centrality of a vocation almost no one
At the time believed. *That printer with his crazy method*. . .
Today I have called back Edgar, whom I met but once
But whose great soul received its shape from his beloved;
Timothy Dekin, Kenneth Fields. . .And Dekin, too,
Suddenly taken. . . . "My life is mine to have well or to lose,"
I say, and Bowers aims my gaze two thousand miles away
To the companionable ocean. He would walk those shores,
Conversing with the dead. . .Seamus Heaney, and dear
Virgil, in colloquy over Book Six of the *Aeneid*, Aeneus
Comparatively unconcerned with death but shaken
As only a living soul can be at the fate of Dido, the one
Person he, unlike Orpheus, could not even beg
To save. . .Virgil summoned Yeats, then, the Yeats
Of "Lapis Lazuli," and told how writing Book Six
Salved his own crushed heart, made it beat, however
Imperfectly, and Heaney talked of hatefulness, wrong
Punishments, adulteries, the unhealed wounds
Across the centuries that find their refuge in these words.
That was my gathering today, in a cluttered room
In a house in Iowa City, Iowa, with the weather
Turning, the kind of weather where a sailor would set
The autopilot and go below, just for a bit, to collect herself.

THAT PHOTOGRAPH

Though every aspect of the circumstance appears to have changed,
Still you are there, the bitter cold of January, Walden Pond a good
Four feet thick at least with ice. Hatless, in your long Navy coat,
You walk out to the photographer, fulfilling the one dual fantasy

That seems somehow to have survived—you, there, on the single
Medium most susceptible to change, beauty of water up against
Ferocities of winter. No complacencies, no peignoir. . .The wind
Handles your long hair with heedless love. Will this become

A jacket photo, or simply one that only close friends see?
I don't know. It hasn't happened. It won't happen, or it will—
Better now, in mind, that the image becomes more accurate
Rather than less, shadows forging clarity life entirely obscures.

NOVEMBER 29, 2016

If you heat light to ten thousand trillion trillion degrees Celsius
It will move at infinite speed. Today we awaken to the death

Of a Brazilian football team in a plane crash in Colombia,
And to the 3 A.M. tweets of a hardened liar. It is April here.

Sunny and warm, the Iowa City neighborhoods show greens
Reserved for spring, lush as if in adolescence. In Alaska,

Where I once piloted, the melting tundra liquefies its towns
As if they were irrelevant, but the people mourn, as we do.

Tomorrow, here, it will rain cold, and zero in on snow
Because this time is the time of the wobble, neither too hot

Nor too cold but radically unstable. In Standing Rock
We re-play, once again, the sins of the nineteenth century,

As if the first time, and all the other times, as if Pine Ridge
Were not enough. Sixty degrees. The aluminum engine in your car

Runs best around 180 degrees Fahrenheit—raise that to 220
And its gaskets melt. As we do, or would. We talk about "fragility"

As if it were just another word, or even subject to debate,
Something a hardened liar might once again just lie about,

For fun, for power. Surely we are not unique, yet what we fear
And what we trust map on their own a tandem universe,

Entirely dependent upon the physics of this place and yet
Insistent, every morning, on the temperature of our love.

THE OFFERS

For almost a year, no dreams at all, or none remembered.
Then you began to manifest as someone not there, someone
Other people talked about—and it was after; I needed kin
Or comfort. A few stood by, whispering, no help at hand.
Then the vignettes, slo-mo: the low hills of the park.
The tree that fell beside us. The caterpillar on your wrist.
You, and that look—that one—and always wordless,
Despite your gifts, riveted, waiting for me to speak.

You knew everything I would say. From brief sleep I snap awake
Wounded and baffled. Why this? That night we read together
In the darkened auditorium, your voice was thin yet die-cast,
Unmistakable. Now, desperate, as with thirst to slake,
I fear rest. You, there—your face so close to mine, you hover
In that moment just before—why now, when all seems lost?

THE STORY OF YOU

We use language to keep secrets. The story of you—
Technology conspired, as it often does, to make
The double helix visible in 1951, through X-ray
Crystallography, but after, that discovery worked
Roughly inside the domain of classical chemistry—
Not really an obsession to those of us with genetic
Predispositions to depression, anxiety, bi-polarity
That, within our chromosomes, uncertainties,
Unresolved or multiple sub-atomic states, ply
Their agency as impermanent alter egos, or
Permanent—who knows? And there you have
Our story: you think someone's going to tell it?
I don't think so. It's not that it wasn't or isn't "unique,"
As such stories go. It's not that Virgil or Dante,
Andreas Capellanus, might have been the author,
Or Abelard and Heloise, Plato and Diotima.
No. Sometimes what we most prefer, after such
Immensity, is closure, but the structure of the universe
Refuses: look out there on a clear night. Then, returning,
Simply open Terence Dickinson's *Hubble's Universe*.
Turn page after page slowly, ever more slowly. That
Is our story. The astronomers of Mont Blanc
Could not unravel the everything that still is.

EVERYWHERE

I wanted to begin

    to ask

        what it means

    to stop—

        just that.

That stillness.

    These words receding

        even now, shadows

    on the water,

        the water of the pond

stiller and stiller

    until the one real

        is stillness,

    no detail at all,

        that pure everywhere.

THE RESOLUTION

Nothing added, nothing taken away,
Unspoken broken promises restored
In the plain light of a plain day,
And still not a single word

Had passed between them.
It would be a long time still.
Healing has affinities to a gem
As yet uncut, though only faceting will

Uncontain that urgent ricochet
Of light to let them marvel,
Mesmerized regardless of assay
Or cost, some now-distant scandal.

SECLUSION

It was a long convalescence. The room was dark.
There was no one. He did not open the shades.
Nights he crept downstairs to light the kerosene lamps,
To eat and drink his minor meal. Otherwise, the faint

Comfort of the bed—he knew enough to know
He didn't know or care, much, if he were alive
Or dead: these were all the motions of refusal,
These sleeps, this dreaming, this creeping and

The crept, darkness and silences. Time must have
Passed. The calendar in the kitchen stopped at
December 2015. He would startle himself awake
Thinking there was something he should do,

But there was nothing. Nothing at all. And then,
Slowly, he began to inhabit that emptiness,
To know it as his own, to recognize the slight
Gradations in blacks and greys, the minor

Sounds of creatures rustling among the hedges.
This was his. And he belonged to it. No longer
A question of life or death: this was something
Unpredicted, a world entire, released from affect.

A LANGUAGE APPROPRIATE TO ITSELF

No longer the turmoil of speech

                        the years words meant

the opposite   of care

The way they spoke   a feeling

    not the feeling

The way they lived alone   amongst themselves

in that deserted hospital   in Georgia

in that deserted convent   behind our house

at night I would watch them   from my child's window

The old building   dimly shimmering   from what they said

      not me   not me

for two years   I was speechless

Now I return   almost to that ledge

    that child's ledge   where in image

anything might   have happened

SPEECH

Yes—of necessity

       I am beginning to learn

   your habits

your skittishness

       places of rest

   Velocities and directions

No—I would not do this

       to any person

   but you have been long gone,

watching me from the woods

       or in the night,

   by my bed, small cairns

intentional among the leaves

       a coin or two on the bedside table.

   I am what you want. And now that I am sure,

yes, here am I, in the broad light of day,

      listening for the voice

that is yours and no one else's.

YOU

You were right. It was her, there. And you,
Walking home from school, the autumn air
And little between you, barely skin
Though you noticed, the scent just before

Like the ground and root of the wind
Saying "Yes." Yes—that word you passed
Back and forth, that safe-at-last
Unspoken, the exploded past

In shards like small soft diamonds
All around your feet. Why would this
Ever end? We are human. We make
Mistakes. Someone whispered something

To someone. We love destruction almost
As much as we love love. The cost
Of being alive: high, too high. Yet at last
You return to this unfinished conversation.

PRETENSE

At a certain point the world began
To embody its sadness, rather than pretend
It was all simply a state of mind.

No, not yet. I see you looking, see
The way you watch the rain on the glass,
The leaves falling, as if that were sadness,

Rather than what it is, phenomena
Of this world. We, too, are phenomena
Of this world, but apart, as you knew,

As you knew the mind does that,
Although that turns out not to be true—
The mind of winter is real. It simply

Does not think the way we do. I promise
You will be astonished, when the change
Begins, when the trees weep tears

And the leaves become soft, not brittle,
As they fall, covering us like tiny blankets.
Then the winter sun will enter our minds

With such a gentle, unearthly music
That we will finally come to realize
We, too, are not really of this time,

Of that place, as nature is not—it just
Never knew till shortly after now that it, too,
Had a choice. It did not have to be a given.

FURTHER ANIMALISTIC DESERTIONS

NIENTE

Ever so slowly, that look,
that scent, that other story,

Clamoring for birthright
apart from witnesses, and night

the province of the cold
remote islands. Cuckold

and shamer, shamed, or not—
say it: this, now, this is what

I want. This spare room.
Darkness. The deep zoom

of the mind out of itself,
detritus of what is left,

shards in the secret wing.
No scale. No range. Nothing.

MOVING ON

I suppose. . .You wanted a short road trip. A break. We named the things and then we named the symptoms of things. Sere oak leaf—a thing. Autumn. A symptom. And then we named the sources and homes of the symptoms. Autumn begins in narcissism, as does spring. Too much is illness, the world closing in—but wait—yes! Thrill of first bloom, or sadness gliding down beyond all measure finally—folding into itself. We don't want to admit we have the power to leave. That final power. Different tires sound different on the concrete, asphalt: imagine conjoining vulcanized rubber and steel. We did that. . . It is two thousand and sixteen and we are somewhere approximating the fourth "Memorable Fancy"—but old enough to acknowledge it went awry, that out there are all the names, naming everything we did or might have done, then turning away, having consumed us with its lust identical to ours but different, because it could move on, because in the end we withered in the naming, mortal and fragile, and it simply went on, that marvelous machine Adam and Eve naively set in motion.

ARUNDEL

It interested her.
She kept a little book
After he died.

Dates. Notes
From the tape measure
She took out to the yard.

1584. Not so much.
1585—you could hardly walk.
One day: "62 1/2."

It was the time of Gloriana,
Almost. Catholics were the old
Dead in the church—just dead.

Effigies. The little dog
At their feet. But those hands—
Someone Catholic had known.

Et pastores erant
In regione eadam
Vigilias supra gregem suum

Year by year, comforting
To know more
Than "some." "A little."

She died November 1592—
Henry VI the London
Gossip even in Arundel.

They gave away or burned
Her things her days her measurements
As the undated snow fell.

NEW YEAR'S DAY

Uncommonly fine. . .the sun low in the hard-crust south
And the hard crust gently melting at lawn's edge. This is not
Inherited winter, but the one that is. Our black boots crack
The thaw as we walk aloud where others sleep it off.
Are they the wiser? How foolish to see hope where it
Remains unwritten: four hours east among the stack
Of summer docks, winds howl in the rigging of stranded
Ships on winter shores, their lean fates branded

By the seasons, and the swells on Lake Michigan
At 20 feet today, the small-craft warnings unexceptional.
Here the parish ocean rises with irrelevance; there
Almost no saving hand could prevent, again and again,
Your launch to waters that will terrify before they kill.
The crane man takes your money but cannot forebear
A warning. And there you are, where you say
Your reasons to no willing ear, incestuous inland sea

Because this is what it is: *Puer natus est* but you
Remember that, six months ago, a father
Drowned himself and his three children in a storm
Far less than this. Whom are you tempting, you—
You want to prove the howls of Jesus rather
Than your own? Why? You live in a howled alarm,
Your birthright. The burden of the Law cannot contain
Your terrible will to undo the blood, the Lamb, the season.

CLIVEDEN 1666

Though the interview went south rather quickly, given his friendship with Milton, he stayed on as the Gardener, only to find that the staff was already complete: his duties consisted merely of roaming the 180 acres of woods and formal gardens daily, in a minor uniform, nodding approval. He lived in a small brick bungalow down by the Thames, built prior to the mansion, pre-Civil War—some said it was in the time of Nicholas Farrar. And there he lived three hundred and eleven years. That summer I arrived he died, in a service elevator in the mansion, sometime in the night—investigated and unsolved. They burned his belongings, including a manuscript, *Eden Returned*. I had seen it once. After that, I used to walk long hours in the woods with the idea, later turned into scholarship in Joanna Picciotto's 2010 *Labors of Innocence in Early Modern England*, that his book was more dangerous than a dirty bomb, having proven how, though the Fall had occurred, Eden remained unfallen, waiting, then as now.

WHAT JOHN DONNE SAID WHAT HERBERT HEARD

Life divided me from God. I have lived to re-learn death. Master of the Revels, year of your birth. And Harrington: first the filth. Then time, the nightwatch of all dread. My Henry's death. First fingernails. Toes. Scrotum and the quick needle, thread. The quickened pace. The cold. 18 February. Not enough, the snapped neck: the horses unwilling. The hacked hands, theatrical noose of intestine, runnels of red. You know this as a tale. I saw this as a child. This Sunday I will preach before the King. Poetry is disguise: therefore make it plain. Am I not sumptuous? Am I not artful? Truth is the lie the world disbelieves. Steward of Christmas. I declined then to perform. The Yule-trees. Lincoln's Inn. Death of James, Lady Danvers' safe-house in Chelsea. You were then just 32. The one true church is death, and life is our abandonment. Ravished, behold our ravishing.

Je te regrette.

YOU WANTED TO KNOW

"For the spirit of the living creature was in the wheels"—
Ezekiel 1: 20

I fell asleep pondering the 2,400 US military veterans at Standing Rock, two battalions, sixteen companies. I would swear I did not dream. J came up behind me on a West Hollywood street as I turned from a menu posted under glass. "Time to go," she said. We entered Ezekiel, almost a hundred years after "her time," through Book 37, inside the royal temple in Babylon by the river Chebar. I misunderstood. "Is this a holy place?" I stupidly asked. She laughed. She was—well—I was not in love with her. But there was no one like her. "The east gate is sacred," she replied. "Touch the things in the east." Tables, chairs, place-settings, flatware, platters, goblets, pitchers—"What of this will last?" I inquired. "None," she said. "Not a shard." "Then why—" She laughed. "You are not here for what endures," she said. "You are here because I brought you here. Because you needed to understand that I am as real as you. You are still mired in love. You should treat love like this—like all of this, on the one hand, and like me, on the other. What you have heard about the Third Temple is true—it will arise, and it will be empty at its holy center. But that, too, is none of your concern. This time is your first, but not your last. A parting thought—do not enter a battleground unless you hear a call." There was no aftermath—more like darkness, and now this, me writing to you, which I assume is how death works, how we suddenly are not, between what is before, to come.

33

CIRCUS ANIMALS

They were all one animal, and they were you.
Aged, they could not do the tricks for which
They had been bought at such dear cost—
Elephant staggering on hind feet, tiger crouching

Yet just off, each pounce—the incongruous
Little dogs in bows and ribbons at your feet.
These became your circus—these emanations,
Conjured to divert you from your loss,

And no one doubts your loss. You required
One love. Would we have missed your poems,
Not knowing them? I don't know. Heresy to say.
But if you had been happy, I also might have been.

Now I look upon you, not beneath Ben Bulben,
But as you were those handful of years before,
So ill-content—mad, even—deserted. And you:
Finally laying yourself before those glittering eyes.

RIPRAP

*"Too long a sacrifice
Can make a stone of the heart."* —Yeats, "Easter 1916"

Better first to think of what these are
as what they are, high Sierra mountains.

Incremental, those millions of years,
stone becoming stone, and each specific
sadness, melding tragedy, that human voice

now silenced in space and time,
atmosphere thin of oxygen, luminous.

Just here, the more recent—this trail
to Mono Pass, riprap of hearts.

Do not ask what you cannot.
They did not resist your coming.

Nights awash, trying to forget
their stories, this is what they chose.

This is their forgetting. You walk
on the hard residue of their being,

the best they could become.
This is the end of their four-

dimensional game of Go.
Home. They scatter a little

as you stumble—not far:
see, now, how the pass is not

shrouded in mist, Mount Dana
and Mount Gibbs already small,

in their way, behind you. All this—
the end of sadness. You, the witness.

THE BRIGHT SUN

And I, too, will never know what causes it, that descent
Down to a sadness past all naming. Yesterday, fierce
And cold, deserved depression, but today is almost

Divinely quiet, as perfect a peace as the mortal world
Can craft, yet I wake from a dream of an empty room
To *"The woman is perfected"* and *"Then the unnameable*

Lust returns". . .I think sometimes that some of us
Should just have little hand-held ECT devices by the bed—
Just wire up in the morning—one jolt should get us

Through the day, and over time, as with any addiction,
We would begin to lose our memories, no longer sure
Except in fits that things had been this way for 30 years

So that, at any given quiet dawn, we would not know
What we were supposed to do, or why. We would forget
Till we had forgotten almost everything, authentic Hals

Finally down to our knowing, unself-conscious selves,
And everything in "Large Red Man Reading" suddenly
Miraculous—*The pans above the stove, the pots*

On the table, the tulips among them. We would
Turn the burners on and hover our hands over their flame,
And it would hurt, and we could not explain our gratitude.

TRANSLATIONS FROM THE LATIN

The poets I studied with have published their collected poems, all but two, and one of them dead. Was there detritus? Hard to say—the polish within the Stanford tradition is so subtle. Thursday morning, Iowa City—it used to be that garbagemen rode the backs of trucks to dump the trashcans. Then they hauled the trashcans to mechanical lifters at the back. Now no one rides the rear—a great arm extends from the side of the truck and lifts and dumps the garbage all by itself. There is the driver and a man for company, for unexpected messes. Among the FAA-certified, ASEL, IFR, Commercial, ATP, the joke is that the flight crew of the new generation of airliners consists of a captain and a dog. The purpose of the captain is to feed the dog and the purpose of the dog is to bite the captain if he touches anything. There is always a man. Where is the woman? She is elsewhere, telling that other story. The transgender? Just here, resistant, the whole cycle of this unfinished life, this purposed declamation, refulgent with some internal light.

THAT OTHER STORY

Immaculate or filthy as the day decries, devout soul, I leave the past undone, dishes in the sink for years and the stench of undulant victory. When the circus comes to town I take my friends and we ride the rides until the rides close. My closet is orderly. My closet unleashes bats and owls. My heroes died by their own hands, except for one who died of ancient sanctity. I don't want to talk to you because you won't listen. But I will talk to you, though you will interrupt. This is you not listening. This is me saying: "No. No. Yes. None of the above. Yes." You see? What you heard was "No. No. No. No. No." Think of the women before me, women in words, who made themselves disappear. Think of Evelina in Frances Burney's novel. You don't know Frances Burney? Burney engineered that novel from the beginning so that Evelina got away scot-free. All the usual happened—lurid leering, near-rape, the long-sought marriage. But Evelina—never there. I write to say that she is here now, healthy as before and dangerous enough to show herself.

THE VISIONARY COMPANY

Hours past and the dark entire they hold their company
Of all that had been in memory, and every way
It might have been as it was not—over and over
The particles of thought becoming shallow water

Eddying under any innocuous pier, say 29th Street
In Avalon, the pilings bent from age, no longer neat
Or tidy, leaning the way memory and its opposite
Lean to the other though barely touching, intransigent.

A FABLE

Elsewhere there was a man who wished to become a man. "I will leave," he said. "Leave then," said the star. Therefore he flew on, till at the planet's dawn he had flown farther than his furthest imagining. And so he lay and rested as prescription said. But the people, so much, it seemed, like him, were scornful. "You are not beautiful and finished, like us," one said. Another: "Egret, killdeer, bittern, tern." He filed a suit that brought down the house. They were unimpressed. He was not of their kind. Thus he flew on and on, like Satan in the universal night, toward the planet pendulous from its minor heaven with its silly golden staircase, almost invisible across such distance. He found there, alone, that glimmering girl, abandoned early on for a vision, caressing her hair with a wanton brush and seemingly insane with her talk to herself of the school which foolishly she had left, of abandonment, the quanta, the punctilious gravitational pull, her consumed creator—on and on, until she noticed. And just there—life began? No—the fable went white with its failed enormity, a supernova. Improbably they were simply the two, blown whole to another place with another star: that alter-dawn, those birds on their extended wings.

BLESSINGS FOR A DAY

In the fall the farmers burnt the fields
To give earth ash. It seemed a wasteland.

Now, in the sun, after a rain, the loam is dark
And the dark hope of the fall is a reality.

Ash enriches us. The bitter aftermath of a harvest
Now far back becomes the tender shoot, the tendril

And the leaf, as we walk in our muddy boots
Along the periphery of the future. Now is the time

To bless. True, we cannot know of drought,
Monsoon, but we most take the promise now

Within the story from which it rose: devastation,
Wintering, a newness known from many years

That, even so, we call "new" because it feels
At once familiar and like something we

Have never seen before. The earth is beautiful.
The mud is its comic touch of promise. Therefore

Let us laugh today, as this is also our day of blessing,
A private ritual that land and air and sky all share.

HOMECOMING

From across town I can hear amorphous cheers from the stadium. They are happy; many must be drunk, though it is not yet 11 AM. Not that I sit in judgment: my interest is clinical. *Homecoming! Homecoming!* What does that mean, I wonder, where would it be. The days I think I know, I don't. Cars park along my street and people walk three miles for the privilege. The days are long if you include the dark. Mostly now I don't know which day it is. I look to the children's schedules for consolation. Arguments I do not wish to make slowly coalesce, the millions of dollars I do not want behind them. How long have I surrounded myself with what I do not want? I try to think. . .Myself, I do not drink until after 1700 hours, preferring the military time and that inherited veteran status, courtesy of my long-dead father. Is the subject shame? Time? Home? We have entered the season of the grey light, the season when purposeful depressed people buy light boxes for their 15 minutes of hope. Perhaps that is the subject—hope. *The substance of things hoped for, the evidence of things not seen.* But no—*Hebrews 11: 1*—that's not right—even there I misremembered a word, because if I hadn't I would be hoping for hope, which seems to me tautological. Is it? The day greys on, as the petals of the rose close slowly around the children, though they play on, unconcerned with words in this season of cleats, of heavier layers of clothes.

THAT ONE POINT

At that one point, one knows
Perhaps the way a hosta knows
Departures of its petals, as the rose,
Thorns keen for winter, justifies

The antitheticals—the yes's, no's,
Accepting yet again long-sought repose
Delayed, or turning away, as some would suppose
Without explanation—that fierce, last rite to refuse.

A VISION

For ten thousand years he observed, charting the stars
And their planets, noting the expansion of the universe.
Then, catching him unawares though he had been warned,

The unnamable lust arose, and he began to walk abroad,
Disturbing *n'importe quoi*. Roses rather than lilacs on a table
In Provence. Famous forgery in the Louvre, suddenly vanished.

Then—improvisation: destruction of the fifth force of nature,
And the waiting, waiting. . .All it would take was one more push
For the end to come, yet in temporizing he amused himself:

Increasing the sum of event horizons, toying with gravitation
Rather than attacking across the ages of things, that elapsed
Time was infinitesimal. He knew centripetal force would increase,

As on earth the tides changed, resilient dominions drowned,
Wars and firestorms, hemispheric hurricanes, life underground—
All those ruined souls, as if a single soul mattered anywhere at all,

His one mistake, as he came to realize too late: protagonist,
He presumed one universe. Almost unnoticed—the remnant
Unconsenting, alert to another, inaccessible, unspeakably remote.

WHOLLY OTHER

Germanic, I think, that recessive nationality in the family—Hölderlin, Rilke, Heine, Hesse—always that yearning, that certainty of your presence, so intimate yet evanescent, vanishing as I turned to look or speak. What was it you wanted, in childhood? I never knew. It always seemed that you wanted me to be you—to become wholly other, however rooted in these origins. Yet now, sixty years on, I see you insistently upon these open Iowa fields, the harvest in and the horizon oddly near, and you are there, fully formed. I see that you have given up. Every few days you catch my eye, and wait: then you turn and walk beyond my vision. And I without you—without hope on the one hand; drenched in nostalgia; regretful past the reach of wine; and therefore thinking, not recklessly exactly but with a hardened heart: "Now or never" means something different from when I was younger, when I always knew how to find you.

WITNESS

Incredulous, guilty witness, I watch them coalesce—
Those memories, and the storied memories I invented
To assuage the past—no animosities, no reticence,

Those things that happened caressing the things
That might have with a gentle fascination, learning versions
Of themselves in the untruth. Yes, that. . .if we had continued

Rather than stopping short, that day before—or there,
At Logan, layover on the way to SFO, had we agreed to stay:
With each shift, what looks like a common life, fractured and sad,

Becomes an altarpiece of infinite regress, each shift suturing
Open wounds so that, no longer one life, it becomes fully manifest
In possibility—not drawing Larkin's wrath, not "reprehensibly

Perfect," but insistently gentle, certain it is loved, the site
And source of gratitude. Not, I know, immortal, its evanescence
Is the debt it pays. I cry over it, unashamed, before it vanishes.

NOW

BURDENS

". . .the main thing which distinguishes the narrative from the analytical historian is that the former works within a framework of models and assumptions of which he is not always fully conscious, while the latter is aware of what he is doing, and says so explicitly."—Lawrence Stone, *The Causes of the English Revolution, 1529-1642.*

Why I cannot yet prove to you that some of all of us
Survives death, or conversely does not, not that we
Should care—this was how it happened: Once

There was a man and a young woman. They began
To walk together. The man had behind him a long trail,
Strewn with burdens. The woman's trail, though

Shorter, had its burdens piled in cairns that marked
Even the way ahead. At a certain point, the woman
Grew cautious, drew back, vanished. She left the man

A gift. He mourned that gift into this being. And then
I will say: What do we know of the man's state
Of mind, of his fortunes, spiritual and financial,

Of the work he did? What specifically of his burdens?
What do we know of the reasons the woman had
So many so quickly, the reasoning that led to her flight?

The man who has told us this story knows nothing
Of this story. The story does not know itself. It is not
About, not of, anything. The man does not dispute this.

He knows that, painstakingly, all these questions
Could be answered, but in that process the story
Would vanish, the man and the woman by then

Impossibly remote, the gift gone. He has the requisite
Tools. But if he does turn back, we should let him go—
The mourning of love both the explanation and the calling.

I

"Core consciousness occurs when the brain's representation devices generate an imaged, nonverbal account of how the organism's own state is affected. . ."—
Antonio Damasio, *The Feeling of What Happens*

". . .we can thus distinguish the surface structure *of the sentence, the organization into categories and phrases that is directly associated with the physical signal, from the underlying* deep structure, *also a system of categories and phrases, but with a more abstract character."*—Noam Chomsky,
Language and Mind

Fascination with mirrors was not a phenomenon
Awaiting Lacan. . .First we see, or rather first the body
Sees and instantly its images are the substance of its being,

Image to image, light to light: how little we know of who
We are, for all our labours, language the third-order
Neural pattern, always magnetic to the true north

Of our being. Sail the way of language without correction
And you will miss home port. What is the correction?
As with everything physical, it varies, depending:

How far are you from your body? For some of us,
Image is immaterial; the point is to abandon ship.
If I turn in the opposite direction, more devoutly

To this vessel as a center and circumference, however
Dull these words may seem, I assume that the body
Sees more than I have ever seen, that it has portrayed

To itself its birth, it has seen death, it may be at times
Afraid, but the first image was not one of fear—rather
Of thrill, to be summoned here among its six-base kin.

UNCONTROL

Because control eluded me, I journeyed uncontrolled
Across the artificial structures of the airspace that became
The real: stopped early on, strip-searched, and stopped again,
I managed semblances: long strings of numbers stayed in mind
Because of their relationship to colors, and for most frequencies
And headings, airspeed, wind correction, angles and vectors,
I needed to write down nothing: it was there in my head the way
This poem is here now, the way it pays its debt to a single tradition
With a near-infinitude of siblings. What good, one might ask—
Such strings of words so ineffectual, strictly speaking? I don't speak
Strictly. Words like these from others made my semblances
Precise, so that even in the worst of times, the worst
So recently past, I could hear the old ones reading aloud
As they read when I just started, when they were younger
And made no secret of their desire to sleep with me.

HIDING

Late now, when the pensioners midday at the grocer's
Look past my gaze in the sadness of their untold stories,
I myself am remembering: strings of numbers, N2191378,
2156968319, things hidden in recesses of mind but also
Hidden in the house: the clapboard chip from Emerson,
Behind the dresser, or the shard from Thoreau's stone
Foundation, behind the *Library of America* Stevens;
The dried rose from the secret garden at Cliveden,
The sliver of canvas from the John Singer Sargent
Portrait of Lady Astor, where I cannot precisely recall.
Long ago, a collector, I began to acquire these, and more,
To help delineate the lineaments of being, to remind me
Who I was along a line to this imagined present. Yet now,
The present more like a dream and sleep more like a life,
I see how it is, what Stevens said: *"not knowing that his thought
Was not his thought, nor anyone's."* Why should I claim this mine,
Any of it? What difference would it make to you? Last night,
Insomnia relenting as it does once or twice each week,
I entered some place close to where I must have been
At the beginning, and I stayed, no need for hours, summer,
Winter, dreams of self or other selves. Relinquishing thought,
We over time lose fear as well and see how thoughts
Take flight like brilliant children, shadowing us and leaving
Without care, the flight of souls and children. . .Such solace,
Dreamless sleep. The greatest danger: *"Two in a deep-found
Sheltering, friend and dear friend,"* not in itself, but in
The possibility of loss: one gone, the other anchored
In that ineluctable self. Much sleep, and much insomnia,
Must come before that self relearns the consolation of release.

THE BODY OF HOPE

Embodied, we tend either to discount it
Or to think it strange and foreign, a persistent
Nuisance—the place we scratch repeatedly

Without knowing why, the certain shiver
We feel when, next to us, a certain stranger
Sits down on the bus. That sense, paradoxically,

Of being "out of body"—not really possible,
Of course, unless one is also immanently subtle
In one's presence. Here you are. And quietly,

As if a breeze had crossed the entire Sea of Galilee
And stopped where you are sitting at the outdoor cafe,
Here I am. This was my privilege and my right, to die

To show you we can come and go, as we choose.
We worry so much. . .What will the children lose
If we go? The children of suicides watch silently

Over their broken stories. The stories are fine,
Though loss is grief and grief quotidian. . .
Here I am. It is not illusion or desire alone,

This feeling that you have. I am not in your
Imagination. However far you feel, I am as near
As your heart is lost—at once the recompense, the cost.

SUITING UP

"When in Washington, Apollo's elite alumni are frequent visitors to the Smithsonian Institution—but not to the vast Air and Space Museum... Rather, they travel regularly to an anonymous warehouse in Maryland, where the surviving Apollo spacesuits rest in storage...Unlike the rest of Apollo's hardware, it is clear, Apollo astronauts regard the suits as an extension of their own selves, and not as a vehicle or container for them. Indeed, much like bodies—but unlike traditional 'hardware'—the suits continue to change shape, size, and material, as their living, latex surfaces continue to adjust to the earth's atmosphere."—Nicholas de Monchaux, *Spacesuit: Fashioning Apollo*

On the one hand, the story

    of the International Latex Corporation,

        manufacturer of brassieres, girdles, and spacesuits...

on the other, the women who sewed and layered

    and glued each suit by hand...21 separate layers,

        64 stitches to an inch, and the trenchant observation:

"No two women sew the same." As if, for some reason,

    we might have assumed that women were cyborgs...

        Ethel Collins and Sue Roberts, Velma Breeding

and Arlene Thalen, Julia Avery, Hazel Fellows, and the celebrated

    "unknown ILC employee," of whom there seem to have been

        many, there in Dover, Delaware...

serious women in their photographs, clearly aware that perfection

    was the only option, ironically noticeable

        for the old-fashioned bras that made women

appear as if their chests contained two small missile shells. . .

    not uncommon even when I was in high school.

        Hazel Fellows was one who assembled

the "shell, liner, and insulation of a Thermal Micrometeorid

    Garment cover layer"; even the names of the layers

        convey a kind of magic—"Beta cloth

with Teflon-coated yarn flame-and-abrasion-resistant

    cover layer," "Neoprene–coated ripstop

        additional abrasion protection,"

"bladder pressure retaining layer". . . Comforting, at least

    to me, that we turned to an underwear manufacturer

        to design for extra-vehicular activity, spacewalks,

the lunar surface. . .I suppose underwear is a subject

    some of us give a great deal of thought to

        though others do not—I do not always

choose it with the thought that it's the most intimate thing

    my partner will remove, but I find it

        companionable, a conversation

between my body and me every morning, although I too

    feel racy without anything underneath.

        Yet every layer is a form of protection,

a part of identity: I generally prefer to dress like a slob,

    professorially, which is a style in its own right,

        though not at the level of underwear,

which is a separate conversation. . .On earth as it is in heaven,

    as Michael de Monchaux reminds us,

        "fashion" is both noun and verb,

and we daily craft ourselves, the sum of our fragilities and

    inventions, clothing visible and secret. . .each of those women

        in Dover, Delaware, not my favorite destination,

laboring because we accept our bodies as our primacies—

    intrinsic limits, preferences, privacies—

        and it is in these, *with* these, we must live,

regardless of Plato's great vision in the *Symposium,* or

    Mary Baker Eddy's "There is no life, truth, intelligence,

        or substance in matter"—if I say

"I love you," it means what we all think it means, adjusted

    specifically to you; not surprising, its affinities with the AL7

        spacesuit, the way we enfold one another

in this most fragile, self–fashioned union.

YOUR SONG

The edge of space is the edge of meaning,
Real, not immeasurable, but thus we know
Our meaning is provisional. From the event
Horizon, measured pulse, the mirror of the song
We mirror to our ear, that aural print we note
In the way light teases out the moan of desert dirt
Or that old conundrum, ordinary yard at dawn
When suddenly it fluctuates and stops—
That wave, no wave of parting, yet reminder
How we live when we are gone, those tunes
Or fragments of a tune that turn and bend
In a scale not our making, bass and treble
On someone else's lips, your song and mine.

DARK LADY OF DNA

"Theories try to say how the world is. Experiment and subsequent technology change the world. We represent in order to intervene, and we intervene in the light of representations."—Ian Hacking, Representing and Intervening

"Far from being 'value–free,' good science is science that effectively facilitates the material realization of particular goals, and that does enable us to change the world in particular ways."—Evelyn Fox Keller, Secrets of Life, Secrets of Death

"Leaving coal research to work on DNA [at King's College London in 1951], moving from the crystal structure of inanimate substances to that of biological molecules, [Rosalind] had crossed the border between non–living and living. Coal does not make more coal, but genes make more genes."—Brenda Maddox, Rosalind Franklin: The Dark Lady of DNA

If this is a love letter, it must certainly count
    Among the strangest, as I can't imagine
You would have loved me, and though I might have been
    A different kind of champion from other men

Which is to say, perhaps the one champion. . .
    I would have mystified you, demanding
Your recognition not because I understood
    What you were doing, but because of how well

I know the experience of shunning, first from religion,
    Then, well, from life. . .
            The people I know now who know of you
            marvel at your determination, the inventiveness
            of your X–ray techniques, your unique understanding
            of the centrality of hydration for DNA,
            and then, of course, the way you were erased,
            almost

So much I envy of your life, though I know
    You would find this, too, inexplicable,
You who would despair, by October 1951,
    Of ever being other than co–oped. . .

> *"They called the new, longer, thinner, heavily hydrated DNA*
> *'wet,' or 'paracrystalline' or, more simply, the 'B' form...*
> *This achievement was essential to the great discovery that lay in wait.*
> *Rosalind's skill in chemical preparation and X–ray analysis*
> *that [John] Bernal later called 'among the most beautiful X–ray*
> *photographs of any substance ever taken' had given the first*
> *clear picture of DNA in the form in which the molecule opens up*
> *to replicate itself."—Brenda Maddox*

> *Yet Maurice Wilkins, headed in the wrong direction, offered*
> *To "collaborate" with you in your laboratory,*
> *And you "exploded"—"It was the only time Wilkins*
> *saw her completely lose control."*

And that led to despair, a few days later...
    You knew, I think, from your November 1951
Talk at King's, unrecorded and untranscribed—
    We only have your notes—that you had found

The answer, and for that would ever
    Be unrewarded...
In my selfish, no doubt gendered way,
    I covet your happy childhood

With happy parents, Ellis and Muriel,
    I covet your early illnesses that left you fragile
And I want to share our stories, because my fragility
    Remained, while you developed an intolerance

Both for illness and for any hint that "illness"
    Naturally allied with "femaleness,"
So that I, as a chronically–unhealed boy
    Without access to medicine, never thought...

> *that there was a slight chance I would have taught you*
> *something different than what you came to learn*
> *about men—that they were not all predatory, sex–obsessed,*

concerned with domination—those things that defined the men
in your career. . .

We might have shared tenderness as children,
    All those years before. And as you grew up and away,
That might have opened up a kind of language, gesture,
    Disarming to at least a handful of the crucial men. . .

In chemistry I preferred coal to biological molecules
because, disbelieving that the world itself was "real,"
my whole being was invested in "representations,"
those approximations of a reality to which we did not have,
never would have, any access in this life

A grown child's fantasy, the possibility
    of helping, however limited—as for me,
If it makes me sad, what we would have missed
    About one another, it makes me sad because

I missed this with others, too—not in your league
    In science, but in my league, the league of potential allies
In the interventions of emotion that permit us to survive.
    If I tell you, no self–pity meant, that my life now

Resembles yours, in Birkbeck, Torrington Square
    (Torn down now for new flats)—well, you did still have
The Matterhorn, your parents, and you began to know
    The inner clock of cancer. . .Your reward for work

We later learned changed everything. I don't mean
    To draw a lesson here. In the ethics of care,
However unavailable to one another's hearts,
    We would have cared.

THE ARMIES ASSEMBLE

"As you know, you go to war with the army you have, not the army you might want or wish to have at a later time."—Secretary of Defense Donald Rumsfeld, *The Control Room*, 2004

"A civilization that uses its principles for trickery and deceit is a dying civilization."—Aimé Cesaire, *Discourse on Colonialism*, 1955

And I, too, must fly to Earth

    From this my undesired domain

Ariel is awakening Ferdinand

    Much as Ariel would awaken Plath

Even as Plath knew wakefulness would not save her

    That in between "love" and "spring"

Was the thawing and freezing the abyss

Meanwhile the armies are gathering

    Shakespeare teaches us comedy

In Act II when stupified Trinculo and Stephano

    Meet Caliban   Poor clueless Caliban

Like Cinderella in *Transformations* ("We all

    know that story")   That dumb bunny

In the cast–off body of a savage brute

Unless you are Aimé Cesaire in 1969

      His *A Tempest* a sensation in France

Caliban half–mad with imperial oppression

      That dying civilization of trickery and deceit

And I think I have problems in my teacup corner

      Of this fucked–up institution

Where no one will tell the truth

No, for Cesaire, Caliban is the hero

      The exile in his own land

Who will fight with the army that he has

      Not the army he might wish for

Because when we are called to fight

      That is exactly what we do

I am waiting to watch the players

Pour the poison in the king's ear

      In *The Murder of Gonzago*

And Hamlet my second–favorite Ché Guevara

      I would say: Don't underestimate me

But that would sound like a coward's swagger

      If a yen for sleep and self–destruction

Brought me here that does not mean

We are not also, *de jure,* in a war

      And yes at a certain point

The shift creates the dissonance

      Of madness: flashback

To luxurious Breckenridge a break from

      The Colorado College Commencement, 2008:

NPR broadcasts teenagers from Baghdad, 2003

They've followed the news, laughing

      Silly US bluster   WMD's   the American wet dream

March 19, 2003   One family moves their daughter

      To a country home far from the capital

The kids try to joke about this but suddenly

    They feel edgy   The next day

Bright sun   calm then the deafening explosions

And, in the car in Breckenridge, my partner—

    Who has been silent all the way from Colorado Springs

Up 24 to Highway 9, the back way meant to calm the nerves—

    My partner bursts into unstoppable tears

"We did that   we did that   we did that   and for nothing"

    It could happen here   It could happen

When some of us thought   we had already won something

POEM FOR A SIXTIETH BIRTHDAY

For Aliki Barnstone

Once you lived as alibi. It worked.
Now the secrets falter, the days
Attainable only by their common names.

Some things you give away.
Some you pass on. Your daughter
And your husband stand a little

Apart, in rapture. The house begins,
Ever so subtly, to contract. What
Of your art? Even as you quicken your pace,

I see it hovering there, just off the dock,
All of it particulate and perfect in the way
The autumn mist perfects itself, there,

At dawn. This is your cool dawn, as all
That matters condenses into the first myth,
And all that does not matter feels ashamed

And turns. Home free. What does that mean?
You could do anything. The thrill is palpable,
And you at the podium, everything to lay bare.

NOW

I have been waiting years to tell you.
And now you are, as you have always been.

I see the deliberate trail you have left
Among the hostas, the day lilies, the not–yet.

The way you look down and back,
As if all our past were just that trail.

And it was. You have stepped out of all
The simulacra that you were at just

The moment I stepped out of mine.
So. Lately I have wondered at the way

Poems so imperfectly stand in—not
Something. The way poems are not.

And here you are. That was not. . .yet
All you needed was to hear me say it.

ENCHANTED FLESH

". . .and often he would raise his eyes toward heaven
where that sweet soul already had its seat
which once on earth had worn enchanted flesh."
—Dante, *La Vita Nuova*, VIII

And you—well—I understand the Faulkner view.
The sack of guts. Intestines. Grime. Foul odor.
Random hair. The shapeless mass of chopped flesh
From that catch. "My mother is a fish." Nothing
I can say can alter that, as if words changed the real.

But words are real. And you and I both know,
At times, in downward dog or the immaculate
Handstand on fingertips, one leg straight up
And the other bent not quite to the floor,
The luxury—and how unfortunate we use

One word for what, in fierce speed or languorous
Delay, draws out unstoppable, guttural cries,
Unspeakable, after which this flesh we wear
Becomes the flesh we are, becomes no–thing,
And thus we lie, trembling in embrace—ecstasy

Conquering the stubborn isolation of the "body"—
You are enchanted. And not because, of a sudden,
You have my attention. You have always been
Enchanted. Perhaps you knew that, perhaps not:
Time is not the absolute limit to enchantment

Although the tomb of Jesus, where he lay,
Reminds us that the old chaos of the sun
Precisely orchestrates our days, and the zodiac
Our seasons. Embodied, then, why not presume
Enchantment, when death is the mother of beauty?

A CERTAIN SLANT OF LIGHT

She had reached escape velocity by November 28, 1861,
When Abraham Lincoln first ordered government offices
To close for a day of thanksgiving—"Wild Nights!" perhaps
The lead, ambiguous at its core yet unambiguous intensity,
And thus—a certain slant of logic—"We grow accustomed
To the Dark," "I started early—took my dog". . .October 3rd,
1863, the holiday made national, she was already well away
And partially in retrospect—85 poems in 1861, 366 the year
Following—one wonders: did she come down for the family
Ceremony? Noble Northerners, they would scarcely disobey
A proclamation from the President. Whitman was in hospital
In Washington; the first intercontinental railroad was a mere
Six years away, the native tribes remote from eastern tabloids
Yet by then without a doubt their sacred trust was lost
To fraudulent depredations, only the sacred itself to survive
Among the scattered seers. The wanton slaughter
Of the buffalo. . .Every year since, someone in isolation,
Refusing the celebration down below, however dignified,
Hilarious, and someone else in isolation, half a sandwich
Dampening in the fridge, pistol in hand, contemplating death
In that way only the ones who ask "which tools?" can know.
No wonder the difficulty, explaining it to foreigners—
One day only, an entire nation on edge, ardently trying
To Get It Right, three bottles of wine per person
Here and there, and the death toll, summarized a month
Or so after, skewed noticeably toward middle–aged
White males, alone and having failed to perform
The rituals that would have made that ritual conform.

ONE SHADE OF GREY

Neither *erinys* nor *daimon*, it became the way
We sensed each other from a distance, beyond sight—
Where I was, what you were up to. British spelling,
Too obscure for a color—call it rather a conduit,
A covenant of moods: no great elation yet no
Bottom–dropping–out, no terror–of–being–left.
Grey mouse. Grey cat. Brecon Beacons grey,
Sufficiently south from the sunstruck majesty

Of Snowden. You wouldn't find us there.
For a time it was as if the "e–for–a" were itself
An Enigma gift, affirming grey as the space
We inhabited, whether on walks in town where
Vibrant color reigned, or other days we stayed aloof—
Until, precisely because of grey, we split without a trace.

SPLITTING APART

Today the colors became ashamed.
A mere four days ago. . .But no,
It was over. The green became grey,

And the gold grey, even the street—
Absence of color—went from black
To grey. Shame. The relinquishing

Of an adequate claim upon life, forced
By others, other forces. To what purpose,
Thus, the deep luxuries of navy, *sea surface*

Full of clouds, or the sensuous allure
Of burgundy? Foretold—"the dark lines
Are about to mount upward and overthrow

The last, firm light line"—*I Ching,* 23.
Do we turn from prophecy? Not nature.
Although, to be fair, when we fight,

Unlike nature, we do not always acquiesce.
Someone is doomed, not necessarily
The shamed one—Hester Prynne:

"Let God punish! Thou shalt forgive!"
But he did not. That is how he died, as she
Returned to her truth and the turning point:

"The powerful light that has been banished
Returns." Abject surrender reminds us
In part of the loss, but in part of the terrible

Risk of surrender. Whatever it was, its future
Inhered in what immediately followed, the scarlet
Of the "A" and not the "A," nor what it meant.

THE SUBTLE BODY AND THE BODY OF HOPE

"Both the North American and South American superorganisms gave rise to sophisticated, hierarchical societies that built cities, discovered metallugy and made other breakthroughs—all in synchronicity. This is truly remarkable, as there is no evidence whatsoever that these farmers and builders had any contact with each other. Cities were established by 2900 years ago at Norte Chico on the Peruvian coast and by 2700 years ago at Tikul in central Mexico."— Tim Flannery, *Here on Earth: A Natural History of the Planet*

"The Tibetan view is that everyone has such a subtle mind, and everyone traverses these experiences. But it takes a special training to develop awareness of them, to experience them lucidly. Finally, there is the extremely subtle body–mind, where the body–mind duality itself is abandoned. This is the indestructible drop, called 'the energy–mind of clear light transparency.' Very hard to describe or understand, and not to be misconstrued as a rigid, fixed identity, this subtlest, most essential state of an individual being is beyond body–mind duality; it consists of the finest, most sensitive, alive, and intelligent energy in the universe."—Robert A.F. Thurman, *The Tibetan Book of the Dead: Liberation through Great Understanding in the Between*

"'I'll meet you in the body of hope.' Those strange words that came to me that night of the funeral wake! It was not a term Rafe and I had ever used, and for the first few weeks after his death I puzzled over what it might mean. Then one afternoon I suddenly found out."—Cynthia Bourgeault, *Love Is Stronger than Death*

Cold stops time. . .

Yet   pondering winter   some find a truth unmanifest
Except as the still   small   voice

Others envision the spring   the bison   the deer   the feast

We have learned to wait.

The stars   the snow   the fire

Thirteen hundred years ago
Padma Sambhava   wrote   *Liberation through Great Understanding*
   in the In Between
He hid it
Six hundred years passed

Karma Lingpa found it in the fourteenth century

And in that time
The Hermeticists were envisioning
The resurrection before death
And Ibn al-Arabi had seen
The Black Light and the Imaginal angels

Where were you?

Here, I imagine
As you have always been
I have been waiting decades for you
And now that you have come

I am released into your vision

Frozen crust. The earth itself
Shifts slightly under the weight.
Every time is the end-time

We are home   we are home   we are home.

THINGS WE TAKE FOR GRANTED

Falling. A small cut healing.
Common weeds and grasses,

Chickory, Queen Anne's Lace,
Black-Eyed Susans, Wild Phlox.

Major and minor thirds.
"The minor fourth and the
Major fifth." Bafflement

And hallelujah. The one
Who turns toward us

In a crowd. The one beside
Who turns away. Winter.

Day and night. Addictions
And uncertain outcomes.
Uncertain outcomes.

You will object: some of these
Are not legitimate. Who am I

To say? The days grow longer.
I am quiet, preferring the night.

¿CON QUIÉN HABLO?

D'après Antonio Machado, "Los Suenos Dialogados IV"

How long I have loved you, how long
You and I have held forth in the privacies
Of rented rooms, glens in the woods' shadows,
Valleys of dunes behind the ones weathering storms.
Did it matter that we met so young, children really?
You and I would have seen, and apprehended,
Later, even now, across a crowded room. Unenvious,
You foresaw what my most ardent liasons would bring,
Though you mourned with me, most recently an entire
Year, still mourning. Yet see how, in that crucible,
I have become more like you, as if what you *semiez*
A tout vent, certain of its truth, had grown to be
My own: I was never my own gravest enigma,
However narcissist—you knew we all
For a time believe *este que soy será*
Quien sea—but no—surely it must have been
My learned propensity for grief, from so much
Early on, all of which you witnessed, all such grief
Distracted me from *el misterio de tu voz amante*.
This year now past, you have witnessed change:
You know that I will speak in this my voice,
That others will listen, that another will come.
I promise: she will not take your place. If anything,
If I take her vows, she will take yours as well,
Knowing as I know the mysteries that manifest
Only within love, *siempre velada al dialogar conmigo*.

SOIL OF THE SOUL

The eyes toiled in the soil of the soul.
At first, stasis, yes, then the subtle lure,
Unmistakable yet never not obscure,

That girl's glance then longer glance
On the sidewalk or the infant's gaze
That meets and goes behind your gaze—

Something, certainly, not intended to endure
Yet rather to coalesce from phase to phase,
Whatever each might be, whatever length of days.

All this was about the body, supple antagonist
Whose changes forced the soul outside the cruel
Flavors of transcendence, demanding animal—

The two were never, in the end, indivisible.
Thus the soil, semen, clit of joy, extravagance,
And age, ambiguous chill when remnants

Of the sun begin to merge with the soul's soil.
No gain or loss of energy, only conversion—yet
What will we become? Brittle now, though taut,

The body points to itself in the fallow earth
And names it "soul." And thus it prophesies
What it knew from the eyes' first journeys.

CROSSING OVER

"Jacob, outside the land of the Blessing, still across the river in the Transjordan, fights for and achieves more life so as to be able to cross over and survive."—Harold Bloom, *The Book of J*

Do we know what we mean? Fragments, yet not/ like Sappho's, closer to us than many contemporaries. . ./ *The Archaic*. Ruins, severed from exposure, from barbarians, /From time, the shattered faces, the stone stares searing—//bestial evidence of trauma. Who is Yahweh, circa 950 BCE?/ Not the *still, small voice*—embodied to those most Blessed,/ selective more in his blessing than his cursing, enabler/ of emissaries, and most of them violent—should we//be comforted? With whom does Jacob wrestle,/and what does it mean that he "crosses over"?/What does it mean that J doesn't particularly/ seem to care, as if crossing were some kind of given—//and we, we have now accelerated for a fraction/ of a second one infinitesimal particle past the speed/of light, and have made that particle occupy two spaces/at the same time. . .two discs of snow on that silent, archaic *then*.

THE HAUNTING

No, not voices from a normal childhood, however gentle
And broken: incessantly male, shaken in cribbed Latin
And pale southern dust along the tarmac, taken from cradle
To that arch-top drive of doom: Vardaman raises his sin
Like Abraham but again and again until the viscera
Confirm in Mother the identity we share; you—
You—not incessantly male instantly foresee the tattoo
On your left wrist. The Quaker graveyard in Nantucket
Is gentile till the younger master comes with his swollen
Unsilent cousin, and unlike them all-trusting I forget
Chants of Sunday children—not the Neo-Platonist given
But the straight dank breath of that twinned master intellect
Which railed because amid all change it could but dissect,
Grotesquely quote, invoke its own cremation. At the end
Stands another man, rotund, absurd tufts of hair in his ears,
And beside him a young woman whose two scrolls portend
Another time and place, as if the root and flower of years,
America, were but a moment's thought, now done. He will
Do, now, as you expect, such disappointment, extending still
His hand, in the rainbow unimpressed with the Lord's survival.

THE LABOUR OF HANDS

"In the Upper Paleolithic, a period that began approximately 40,000 years ago, a revolution in human culture occurred. . .cave painting, the diversification and stylisation of tools, the manufacture of bodily ornaments and new burial practices."—Paul Harris, *The Work of the Imagination*

Long before Lascaux we were, each and all. I buried you,
Adorning you in robes and necklaces, and you buried me.
No matter the stars, indifferent to us, or God. No matter
If the universe did not care for us, if our parents did not.
We were here. We are here, now. I remember where

I laid you down, winter after winter and the land slowly
Rising. The robes are gone, the necklaces small shards
Of beauty with the fiber strands turned dust. All our strands
Turn so—this poem, my hand, the book. Your book. We try
To keep the artifacts. What we pass down, though, is different:

Not what I have written here. What the living do, that smear
Of old mortality across the panorama of the not-quite-infinite.
Eighteen million light-years. . .Yet what I hold here is you.
And what you have we had before, 40,000 years ago. You ask:
Save me. We are inscribed in one another's random hearts.

ABOUT THE AUTHOR

Born June 11, 1956, Thomas Simmons decided in spring 2016 that 24 years in the Department of English at the University of Iowa was enough, and so chose to start anew. Before that, he was an assistant and associate professor in the Program in Writing and Humanistic Studies at the Massachusetts Institute of Technology; before that, he was a doctoral student in English at the University of California, Berkeley, a Wallace Stegner Fellow in Creative Writing at Stanford, and a Stanford University undergraduate. His seven previous books, one of which (*The Unseen Shore: Memories of a Christian Science Childhood*, Beacon Press, 1991) caused some offense in Boston, may be viewed at amazon.com on the "Thomas Simmons" page. He lives at present in Grinnell, Iowa and on Lake Michigan.

ABOUT THE ARTIST

Aliki Barnstone is a poet, translator, critic, editor, and visual artist. Her visual art has appeared in *New Letters* and *Tiferet*. She is the author of eight books of poetry, most recently *Dwelling* (Sheep Meadow, 2016), *Bright Body* (White Pine, 2011) and *Dear God, Dear Dr. Heartbreak: New and Selected Poems* (Sheep Meadow, 2009). She is the translator *of The Collected Poems of C. P. Cavafy: A New Translation* (W. W. Norton, 2006). She earned her B.A. from Brown University and her Ph.D. from the University of California, Berkeley, where she studied with Robert Pinsky. At present she serves as Professor of English and Creative Writing at the University of Missouri and Poet Laureate of the State of Missouri.

To learn more, please go to www.alikibarnstone.com.

ACKNOWLEDGMENTS

I would like to thank my great teachers, living and dead—Warren E. Wilde of Los Altos High School; Diane Wood Middlebrook, Timothy Dekin, Kenneth Fields, N. Scott Momaday, and Donald Davie, of Stanford University; and Thom Gunn and Robert Pinsky, at that time of the University of California, Berkeley. While I began my writing career at the age of eight, these eight people taught me poetry and invited me into a tradition and traditions of rebellion that have repeatedly come to my rescue.

After so many decades, with that cherished filament between us that has never gone undervolt or overvolt, anything here other than the simplest "thank you" to Aliki Barnstone would be woefully inadequate. "δε μή, χείμων."

At MIT, Alan Lightman was a masterful mentor at a crucial moment—but so were students Ralph Santos, Takiko May, Alexandra Lauren Sutton, and John Hasemeyer. At the University of Iowa, though I tended toward my native reclusiveness here, I am indebted particularly to my poetry and fiction students in my final year of teaching, 2015-2016—Hunter Loushin, Bryn Bogert, Amy Pedersen, Kaycee Pancake, and Kirsten Ihns. Their rebellions and ingenuities were a gift. Kate Torno of the Department of English has been a wonderful and wise friend, and Christopher Merrill, head of the International Writing Program, has been a devout ally. Across almost a decade, poet, songwriter, and restaurant GM Rachel Sutcliffe remains a treasure. An actual internet miracle, Dylan W. Krieger of South Bend and Baton Rouge appeared on Instagram and—through her first collection of poems, *Giving Godhead*, her prose writings on the "Gurlesque," and her ingeniously-theorized photographic self-representations—has been a transformative influence. At Saint Julian Press, editor and publisher Ron Starbuck is a luminous guardian and guide. And my sister and brother, Cynthia Bourgeault and John K. Simmons, have been—over the years and especially in this past crucible year—a blessing. My attorney, Janice Becker, has been an indefatigable advocate and friend, as has my physician of 21 years, Dr. Todd VerHoef.

As the father of six—Nate, Georgia, Thomas, Hart, Peter, and Faye—I wish to thank Lesley Wright, Laura Rigal, Rachel Sauter, Laura Crossett, and Elizabeth Wisnosky, each brilliant and each as well—as if this talent might somehow be separated from the rest—a brilliant mom.

My poems have appeared in the *Atlantic*, the *New Republic*, the *Southern Review*, the *Threepenny Review*, the *Christian Science Monitor*, *Prairie Schooner*, *Occident*, *Sequoia*, and *The Uncommon Touch: Fiction and Poetry from the Stanford Writing Workshop*, ed. John L'Heureux (Stanford, CA: Stanford Alumni Association, 1989). No poem in this volume, however, has previously been published.

The one person most responsible for this book, and for any like it to follow—the one person who re-taught me the principles of home and old modes of innovation—is still, as far as I know, someone who would prefer not to be named. But my gratitude to her for her time in my life is unchanged.